# TUFFY

## THE DOG WHO CHANGED MY LIFE

ANIKET G. NITURKAR

ISBN 979-888591065-1

*This book is dedicated to my beloved dog Tuffy*

# Contents

# Preface

In this book I have discussed about how my life got changed after I met a dog.

The dog who completed my life, who had the ability to turn my sadness into happiness, yes his name was tuffy.In this book i have mentioned some tragic incidents which happened with me and tuffy and elaborated it

Tuffy was and always will be alive in my heart forever

The story written is true and the incidents are happened actually

CHAPTER ONE

# Cousins

It was a normal day, I was sleeping like hell it was around 8 AM in the morning thereafter I heard the voice of mom, Aniket wake up your cousins are on their way to home. I was feeling very sleepy and ignored mom, then the bell rang and there came a mumbling sound of good morning masi it was my cousins Nikhil and vaishnavi along with their mom and dad, means for me my uncle and aunt. Nikhil came directly on my bed and started irritating me to wake me up. Hey wake up brother I literally came all the way from Karnataka and you are still sleeping and he took away my blanket harshly.

I felt like slapping him but controlled" hey you dumb ass get out of here right now, I said

Nikhil laughed and went to brush his teeth.

That mumbling sound of talking irritated me then a voice came aniket wake up now it's too late it was dad's sound surely he came from morning walk and I woke up.

However I was happy seeing my cousins at home it's just that he nikhil tried to wake me up while I was sleeping.

Actually this was the time when I myself was 14 years old kid studying in 8$^{th}$ standard. Both nikhil and vaishnavi were younger to me.

I had two elder sisters I was the youngest in my family and hence everyone's favorite. Due to which most of my demands were fulfilled either by my parents or by my sisters. This was a huge advantage for me being a kid I enjoyed this luxury.

Basically I belonged to a middle class family grew up in Aurangabad a city located in Maharashtra state of India. My dad was a government officer in Government medical college Aurangabad and mom was teacher in a convent school both mom and dad had decent salaries.

And the things which were told to me by parents while growing up were as usual as a typical Maharashtrian parents study hard get admission to engineering or Mbbs college get a good job and die, strange but true.

Never the less I had different plans

CHAPTER TWO

# The School

Bhaiyya (elder brother) last year when I came here you said you will have a pet dog, where is the dog? Nikhil asked

Listen bro ill surely have one, I replied

Everybody knew I love dogs we had 5-6 stray dogs in our colony and we used to feed them in the morning and evening

In the evening while I came back from school I used to play with these dogs they were my real friends who used to love me irrespective of my marks in school.

The next day I woke up late, as usual had to hurry up to go to school.

Mom was shouting, I had a bath and did breakfast alone & went to school.

*School:*

Teacher 'good morning class'

Good morning teacher, students replied

So let's start with our new lesson take out your textbooks everyone

Hey Aniket you brought your textbook, Nik Jadhav (my best friend)

Nik shouted from the last bench and I was on the 1st bench

Yes bro,I replied

Usually I and Nikhil used to sit on same desk but that day I was late to school however there was a vacant place on the last bench besides him

Aniket ohh aniket I heard a soft sound while ma'am was busy in attendance

Come on the last bench we will sit together there is a good news I need to share with you immediately,

It was a risky task but had to go otherwise whole period I will get bored alone

I passed on the bag bend down and ran straight away behind ma'am didn't saw me

Yes bro what is it? My sister brought a puppy yesterday and dad allowed to keep him

That's a great news Nik congrats bro, thanks

I had a great talk with Nik all over the school period however in my mind I was thinking I should also get a dog

Soon then it was 1PM o'clock bell rang and we all were ready to go home.

Just while riding my bicycle to home I heard a sound of puppy a very minute sound as if he was very hungry.

I stopped the bicycle and searched for the exact location of sound, it came from the garden located on my LHS where I stopped my bicycle

I parked my bicycle and went inside the garden

And waooo what i saw was just mesmerizing there were around 6-7 Labrador retriever puppies besides there was a huge Labrador female with whom they were playing

And the gardener was feeding to that female Labrador I went to him

Uncle are these your dogs?

Yes little boy he replied

In my mind I was thinking I just want one puppy out of this they are so cutie, uncle are you going to keep all of this puppies with you? I asked

Gardener came to me and said no but what do want exactly just tell me

I want one of these puppies

Yes you can just get 5000rs and take one of them.

I was shocked this was the1[st] time I realized people sell dogs also. I was disappointed I knew my parents won't allow me to keep a dog they never liked it and so it was impossible to convince them for 5000rs

And I sat there for a few minutes I was disturbed. I thought that small sound must be of these puppies

But still the sound came and these puppies were playing in front of me

I went inside the garden there was a garbage place where all the leafs and dirt found in garden would be accumulated as soon as I get closer to this place the sound increased

Yes I am there

And a saw a skinny little very tiny and thin puppy of white tone color there was no one around

Omg he is alone and he was just making crying sound as if he was lost by his companions

Uuuu come here puppy I took him into arms and went to the gardener

In front of gardeners house I saw a man, lady and a boy with them, after listening to their talks I came to know

they were a family and came to the gardener to buy that cute little Labrador puppy.

Such cute babies they all are dad

Yes son, replied his dad (with full of joys)

The family looked very rich as they had their four wheeler with them I thought this is the perfect family for this puppy in my arms as my family would not allow me to keep him.

And after all this gardener is taking care of the Labrador puppies and one day or the other

people will come and buy them all one by one but who will take care of this puppy in my arms (I thought)

Excuse me uncle

Yes boy, he replied

Uncle do you all came to buy this Labrador puppy?

Yes beta my son loves dogs and we all do, so we decided to have this Labrador.

Till this the gardener came out of his house and was listening to our conversation

Uncle actually I found this cute puppy inside the garden, he was crying may be he is alone because I didn't saw anyone nearby

Uncle will you please adopt him it will make his life

He just saw the puppy and said straight away said no to me also his family gave me a strange reaction

The gardener came to me,

Hey you little boy go away from here they are my customers don't try to act smart okay it will be good for you

But uncle what about this puppy he is alone and my family won't allow me to keep him

Do whatever you want to just get lost

I was surprised with the behavior of this people

The puppy was very silent and was shivering of fear and was hungry as well

I took him in one hand and with the other hand my bicycle I just walked towards home

In my pocket I had 10rs note as home was further away I took a milk bag from the grocery shop besides the garden

As it was 2PM it was quite hot I found a tree below which there was a place to sit and shade as well

I took puppy there parked my bicycle, I just opened my lunch box it was empty as I had lunch in school

Poured the milk in it and kept puppy in front of box

The puppy firstly didn't even tried to taste it but within 1-2 min's as soon as he recognized the milk he started drinking it.

I thought I should go now his mother will find him but still my heart was not ready to keep him alone

I just sat with him for a few minutes I had a huge smile on my face, took the puppy into my arms and looked into his eyes there was so much of innocence and I just yelled my "younger brother" and just kissed his forehead.

This was the point I decided I will take him home and he will live with me whatever may be the parents decision I will anyhow convince them.

I started walking towards home in one hand puppy and on the other hand bicycle it was very difficult but somehow I managed.

As I reached home there was no one outside I slowly opened the main gate parked my bicycle and went to terrace and kept the puppy there.

Till know he had a bit of trust on me as I spent a good time with him

Hey kid you be here only till I come back okay? (I said to puppy)

He had milk so till now there was no need to feed him I went downstairs and got fresh

Aniket how come you are late today, mom asked

Umm mummy actually, and I said nothing

I was confused from where to start

Nikhil my cousin who was watching T.V

Suddenly Nikhil said mausi (to my mother)I can here sound of puppy crying

Yes beta I too can hear it and it is very clear now

Mom mom , yes aniket firstly just check from where this sound is coming

Mom I brought a puppy, I said

Omg where is he bhaiyya? Nikhil (overjoyed)

He is on the terrace (me in very low tone)

And we both ran upstairs

Aniket listen to me I want him out of the house right now did you listen to me?? I said right now

No way mumma

As soon as I opened the door of terrace puppy stopped crying

Hey cutie come here, bhaiyya where did you get him?

It's a long story brother I'll tell you afterwards

Around 1-2 hours I and nikhil played with the puppy and now he was very comfortable with us

Mom came upstairs she had a bowl in her hand full of milk, Aniket just give him this milk he must be hungry

I was surprised I thought mom will scold me but this was something unexpected surely because there were guest in house

Aaahhaa such a cute puppy, mausi came

Sister just let him stay he is so cute, mausi said to mom

There was a little smile on moms face she didn't said yes yet but I understood it is yes

Now the main thing was to convince dad

I decided to tell dad everything what had happened

It was 4PM we took the puppy downstairs

As soon as we started running puppy would run behind us this is how we started playing with him

My both the elder sisters came from college and herd me and nikhil shouting

Run run bhaiyya he will catch you, nikhil

My sisters were on main entrance gate and just saw both of us playing with puppy

Hey didi see who's here

Yes we saw him (In a little angry tone)

Both of my sisters didn't liked dogs too much because they were scared of them

This is the most common fear or misunderstanding of people they think that the dogs can bite anytime and that too off without any reason

Hey aniket just hold that puppy there till we go inside

Are you scared of him didi (laughs)

Hey don't act smart okay

And both of my sisters went inside

At 5:30 PM

Dad came from the office as soon as dad opened the main gate the puppy ran towards dad and started jumping on dad

The puppy was In full of playing mood

I was watching all of this through our window dad closed the gate didn't said anything

I brought a glass of water for dad

Dad would you like to have water

Sure son and can I know who brought this puppy here

I told the whole story to dad mom was also listening

Papa please he don't have anyone can we please adopt him?

Dad looked at puppy and said okay we will keep him with us

And I just couldn't believed this

That was probably the best day of my life as I felt now my family is complete.

And there was a magic in his (puppies) eyes every person who saw mesmerized into them

But there's a condition

Yes dad what is it?

You'll have to take care of him

Yes papa I will (Smiles)

Nikhil brought a small ball from nearby shop and we started playing with the puppy

Around 9:00PM

Mom called all of us for dinner

Aniket come here fast

Mom grinded some biscuits in mixer mixed them in milk and poured them in the bowl

Aniket take this and remember from now onward that puppy is member of our family so before you take your meal make sure you feed him first

Now go take this bowl and feed him

I was surprised mom actually started treating puppy like her own son and this was a very good sign

Finally the family which didn't liked dogs are now liking them

I fed him food he ate and slept in our garden

After dinner there were lots of masti going on inside house as my cousins were there sisters and mausi and these are the beautiful times we spend with our dear ones

However before sleeping everyone asked what should we call him?

And the first name came on my lips was "tuffy"

Yes the "hum aapke hai kaun" wala dog

The salman khan and madhuri dixit starred bollywood movie

Around 11PM everyone was in their rooms and I thought of sleeping near to tuffy

So that he won't feel alone

But as I couldn't take him inside our house again "the typical maharashtrian middle class family thing" It was not allowed

However he was kept in a small garden which was inside our compound wall, and was completely secured from street dogs.

Our garden was visible through one of our living rooms window, and we had our sofa placed just beside that particular window

So I slept on sofa that night.

I slept around 11:30 PM

After sometime I just woke up and heard tuffy crying loudly I saw the watch it was around 1AM

I switched on the lights opened the window and saw towards him

And as soon as he saw me he stopped crying.

And now he (tuffy) started running in garden and was playing with the branches of trees I said *chup bass re*( be quite in Marathi) let me sleep now

Then I thought he might be hungry therefore he must be crying

I slowly went into the kitchen without making any noise like a professional thief

I silently took the milk from the refrigerator & closed the door with ease.

Took the milk in a bowl mixed some biscuits in it the Parle-G & took an extra packet so that if he feels hungry he will eat it himself.

As soon as I opened the door of living room tuffy saw me and he came running towards me

As if I was his own family and this was just the same day not even a complete day that we were together and he completely trusted me and it was seen in his eyes, and at that point of time I felt him.

I served him milk and biscuits however he didn't ate.

He wasn't hungry at all just wanted someone to be with him all the time.

And I was feeling sleepy

As soon as I went inside within 5-10 mins he again started crying, And I was like

*"Arey yaar abb kya karu"*

What should I do now

I took a decision (laughs)

I opened the living room door again no sounds at all, but the door still made a slight sound it needed oiling I guessed

Anyways,

Tuffy wasn't able to climb on the stairs so he wasn't able to come to the door

It was now 2 AM and I was still outside the house with him.

I was just observing him and he was such a notorious child trying to play with everything around by god's grace all our footwear's were above the stairs where tuffy wasn't able come so they were safe otherwise it would just have been a disaster.

However he wasn't ready to sleep alone I took him inside the house & kept him on the carpet inside our living room.

On the next day I woke up early before mom I knew I need to keep tuffy in the garden again before anybody in the house knows about it.

So I woke up at 6AM everyone was sleeping tuffy too was sleeping

I took him into arms and kept him in garden he was still in deep sleep & I went back inside

I thought yes I have done it and then I got to smell something when I saw around the living room

Tuffy had peed on 4-5 different places in living room.

Shitt man...! Now I needed to clean it immediately before someone wakes up especially Mom

I immediately cleaned it before anyone could see

Really it's a difficult task to have a pet especially when there are certain constraints in your house.

I didn't go to school that day.

I wanted to play with tuffy and as my cousin (nikhil) was also there

So I made a very common excuse that most of us usually used to make of stomach pain

However it wasn't a big deal I stayed home after asking dad.

As soon as dad went to office I and nikhil started playing with tuffy

Till now he understood that we call him tuffy so now he used to react if someone calls him by that name

As we used call him he used to run behind us

We kept on running inside our compound wall across the built area, sometimes we used to hide somewhere and call him then tuffy would find out from where the sound is coming

So that's how we started playing with him

If I had to describe tuffy he was a typical Indian breed dog with white tone color.

At this stage in life I was very happy and life became so joyful that I cannot describe in words

Tuffy had completely changed my life; I used to care a lot for him and used to treat him like my younger brother.

In the evening I took tuffy to the nearby playground where all my friends used to play

I introduced tuffy to all of my friends and everyone was exited to meet him

Tuffy became more familiar and comfortable with humans now

I could even notice in his eyes that he was surely enjoying his life and so was I with him

When we came back home dad had brought a huge box in which there was a soft cotton placed everywhere inside it

Tuffy was so small in size and therefore could easily sleep into that box at night

Now at home tuffy was given 1st priority that too ahead of me (laughs)

The day came when my aunt,uncle and my cousins nikhil and vaishnavi were leaving for Karnataka

Nikhil, bhaiyya please take care of tuffy he is really a nice dog

Mausi, Yes and don't hesitate to call if your mom scolds you (laughs)

They all kissed tuffy and took photographs with him before leaving

Obviously tuffy would now miss nkhil because when I used to go to school nikhil used to entertain him all the time

And from now onwards when I will go to school tuffy would be all alone

Bye to all ,nikhil

Bye bye brother I said

CHAPTER THREE

# Our Colony

Till now everyone in our colony was aware of the news that we adopted a puppy

I lived in a colony where most of the colony members were dog lovers.

We already had 5 to 6 stray dogs in our colony and the peoples living in colony used to feed them 2 times a day

As these dogs were familiar with me and within a few days they became familiar with tuffy too

By watching tuffy mixing with these dogs all of us were now free of tension as now we were confident enough they won't harm him if in case we are not around

Tuffy was clever enough he managed to spend time till I come back home from school and very quickly he was adopting the things

Tuffy would spend his time roaming in the compound, running behind mom when she used to come outside to water the plants.

Around 5 PM

I sat along tuffy in our garden just one sided chatting with him and he started biting me

I heard the sound of gate

It was dad

Aniket come take this bag beta, yes papa I replied

I brought some toys for him to play just open and give it to him

Do dogs also have separate toys?? I asked

Yes dad replied

I was surprised I just took out a packet that contained a bone like structured toy

Hey tuffy catch this

Tuffy took that bone in mouth and started chewing it

Now he won't bite you, said dad

Papa my friend told about vaccination when should we take tuffy to the veterinarian?

Tuffy hasn't yet completed 90 months as he looks quite younger surely within next 30 -45 days we will vaccinate him son

Okay papa...!

CHAPTER FOUR

# He saved us

Good morning aniket, wake up now time to go to school

Yess mom, I woke up it was slightly sunny outside and very pleasant

I did my daily routine mom was busy in cooking food for my lunch box

At the time I was wearing uniform I heard sound “bhow bhow”

Yes it was tuffy

This time it was a strange bark as if he was trying to say something

He was barking continuously and I understood it is definitely different than his usual bark

I tried to figure out what happened to him

I moved aside the curtain of window, I saw tuffy barking in the garden but it wasn’t visible to whom he was barking

Mom, aniket just see what happened to him

Yes mumma, I replied

I went outside and my eyes were stubbed, I was literally frightened and within sec I was shivering

Yes it was a snake that too huge one

Without wasting time I immediately removed the hook to which tuffy was tied

And the snake was looking at me like a hell

It was a horrible site

I pulled tuffy gently and he understood, as soon as he found his rope was free he ran towards me

He just jumped on me

I took him inside the house and locked the door immediately

Dad dad dad I shouted

Yes what happened aniket?

Dad there's the snake in our garden

Everyone in the house came to see how the snake looks

My dad immediately called "sarpamitra" the snake charmer

The snake charmer came within 15-20 mins till then we all kept a watch on the snake through the window

My sisters were just interested to see how large the snake is

Tuffy bhow bhow bhow in angry tone

Our neighbours gathered in their respective balcony and were egar to see the snake

The snake however wounded himself on one of the branches of the tree in our garden

The snake charmer carefully dragged the snake and just holded in single hand and showed him to us and to the colony members

Everyone clapped for the brave man

We then went outside

What do you guys do to such snakes now?

Hope you don't harm them, I asked to snake charmer

No child,

We very carefully leave them in a dense forest where they could easily find their needs and can further live their lives

That's the reason we are called "*Sarpamitra*" the "snakefriend"

Thankyou for calling me you don't need to panic now

Thankyou uncle, I said

The snake charmer took his fees and went

Between all these chaoses my school was missed & tuffy went inside the garden and still he was barking as if snake was still there

I am really proud of this baby dog now, said dad

Yes he is very clever, mom replied

Tuffy literally saved us all as there was the possibility that snake could have entered our house easily if tuffy would not be there

And it would have been very scary if that would have happened.

The first time dad took tuffy up in his arms and kissed him on his forehead.

CHAPTER FIVE

# The scary night

The mystery of ghost, horror stories are often the most interesting topics which we discuss a lot with the friends in school

Then let it be the mid age or adult this topic is interesting for everyone

The next day in our school our English subject teacher was on leave so we got games period that day

However we didn't had the equipments to play due to some reasons, so we 3-4 friends started discussing about the ghosts

Are ghost real?

Do they really exist in this world?

Do they harm humans?

And numerous questions were there in our minds being a kid I always wanted to get all the answers related to this questions

But I never wanted to be scary about this

Isn't it interesting till the time we forget about ghost we live normally and the time we watch horror movie or listen to some story we feel scary for some days, the same incident happened with me that day

Nik, hey do you guys know dogs can see ghosts

What?

Are you serious bro?

How is that possible?

Three of us asked him

Yes, I am serious

It is said that dogs have $6^{th}$ sense

Where we as humans have only 5 senses

And nik started explaining his point of view on it

However I didn't believed in such stories but it was scary and I actually started being a little scared from that day

At that night something strange happened

I usually used to pay attention to tuffy but that day at night I was more cautious

Many questions were floating in my mind I was thinking that, if it is the case that dogs can see ghosts then tuffy also might can see

Around 9PM

Tuffy come here bro I have brought food for you

Tuffy was sleeping, just woked up listening my voice and started jumping on my legs as he saw the bowl in my hand filled with his favorite food doodh roti.

And also I placed some extra biscuits so that if he feels hungry he can eat it.

Around 11PM I slept in the living room as usual, while everyone slept in their respective bedrooms

Now tuffy was clever enough to sleep alone he wasn't crying at night anymore but I just wanted to know if really can he see the ghosts.

I slept there on sofa placed beside the window through which tuffy was easily visible.

However the curiosity didn't let me sleep that day.

Around 12:30 PM

I heard tuffy, he started barking and I wasn't completely conscious I was feeling sleepy

I woke up due to his continuous bark and opened the window slowly

And what I saw was tuffy was barking to a wall and there was no one else

There was literally no one

Immediately I thought of what nik had said in school

Is it something that tuffy is able to see and I am not?

I was scared that night, is it really the ghost?

Several questions remained unanswered
However the mystery continued as humans haven't yet found proof about ghost.

CHAPTER SIX

# Picnic

It was Sunday thereafter everyone had free time

Dad and mom woke up early in the morning at 6AM

We had planned a trip to Mhaismal Hill station located nearby Aurangabad

We had our own maruti Suzuki wagnor car in which we used to travel

There was no one at home to take care of tuffy hence we decided to take him with us

As dad said tuffy will come with us I was very happy

Till now my both sisters were familiar with tuffy and so he was.

Tuffy in the whole journey was either in my arms or on the seat beside me, however he was so obsessed with the window he just wanted to be in my arms and see outside the window and bark loudly

As he could see different animals that he wasn't much aware of like cows, buffalos, goats, chickens etc

He used to just bark continuously by seeing them

Before reaching mhaisamal there was a small waterfall

Dad can we stop here for a few minutes? I asked

Yes beta, dad replied

Dad stopped the car

Me and tuffy came out of the car immediately

Yay tuffy waterfall, he was absolute in joy when he saw waterfall

Just roaming here and there the land was wet & was full of greenery everywhere around and the sun was dim that day.

Tuffy just roamed like a bird flies in the sky when it is released out of a cage and was playing with water

It could be seen he was enjoying so much

The other families there were amused by watching tuffy.

Ohhh...! Mom look over there such a cute puppy, said one of the kid over there to his mom

By then 3-4 kids came and took a photograph with tuffy as if he was a celebrity

However he was super cute

And till now everyone in family was feeling hungry, except tuffy he was in his own mood

Tuffy come here, come fast my boy

And here he was jumped inside the car

Wait you dirty fellow I need to clean you

*"Bhow Bhow"* only word he could talk

It was now approx 10 km to reach mhaismal, tuffy liked to just see outside the window & bark at strangers

And then we reached our destination.

Tuffy again jumped outside the car as soon as I opened the door

But this time I had his belt in my hand as it was hill station anything could happen hence for safety I grabbed his belt in my hand

After walking a distance inside we reached the view point

And I was just mesmerized and so was tuffy by watching a view through the top

We did lunch over there sitting below one of the tree, and I had also carried his dog food to feed him

People over there watched us

Oh see there's such a cute puppy with them, one of the kids over there

We all enjoyed whole day and then late night we reached our house

And all went to sleep including tuffy as everyone was tired.

CHAPTER SEVEN

# He was clever now

Tuffy became clever now; we both had a great bonding.

I treated him as my younger baby brother, he understood now we all are his family.

Mom was quite surprised as tuffy started protecting his family means us very early

He started to bark at strangers a lot, he used to bark like a hell

And he cleverly new the milkman, who used to deliver milk at our house so there, was not point he could bark at him any way

People in the colony started recognizing the dog is becoming hell danger in terms of protecting the family

So we had no fear of theft in future we assumed once tuffy will be fully grown up he will ensure no theft occurs here

However he could also recognize the daily kids playing in front of our house and he too used to sometimes play with them

Shaking his tail he would urge people of the colony to play with him sometime

Papa used to take tuffy to the walk at the evening

Now he was nearly two months old the colony dogs became his friends now

So we used to send him to play with them for a few minutes

He used to come back at home himself after some time

Tuffy became much healthier and attractive everyone would adore him now.

CHAPTER EIGHT

# I can't lose him

It was routine day, I came back from school parked my bicycle

Tuffy where are you baby,

*Bhow Bhow,* and he came running to me

Mom came, Aniket firstly you go get fresh have your meal and then play with him, he is also hungry let him also take his meal

Ok mummy, I replied

Hey you, little kid have your meal I'll be back

However tuffy didn't understood (laughs)

I had my lunch came back to play with him, but tuffy had slept as soon as he had his meal

He was use to the routine now

At 5 PM

Wake up tuffy, come on we will go to the park boy

And tuffy started jumping on me, took his leash in my hand and we started walking towards the park

While going towards the park tuffy started barking to the stranger dogs, he was literally barking to the much elder dogs than him

And I was like what a confidence he has now than the previous nervous tuffy when 1$^{st}$ time I saw him

As we were about to reach the park tuffy saw sisters ashwini and anuhar coming from college as there was the bus stop their bus just had arrived

And tuffy recognized both of them from a very long distance and he went running towards them

Hey tuffy were are you going, asked ashwini didi

We are going to the park, I replied

And tuffy was jumping with joy on both of them

And I was amazed by my sisters behavior once they were afraid of dogs even puppies and now they were so much friendly with tuffy

But yes this is called bonding; this is what we call a family

Till now I was able to sense that my whole family was emotionally connected to tuffy

Even the people who never liked dogs were caring so much about him

And then tuffy wasn't interested in coming with me so he went back to home with my sisters

However I went to the park as my friends were waiting for me to start the game

Around 7:30PM

I came back home had dinner with family and fed to tuffy also his favorite rice and milk

Tuffy just loved the combination of rice and milk

Everyone went to sleep at around 10PM

And then at around 11 PM a shocking incident happened

I heard a loud noise of crying of dog and it was surely tuffy

I immediately opened the main door and ran to see him

Mom, dad, my sisters they too came out hurriedly

I was not able to understand what's going on

What just I saw was horrible, tuffy's neck got stuck very badly

All the people of our society came

Everybody had gathered around to save tuffy's life

He got stuck so badly that he wasn't even able to breathe properly

I was shivering scared as my baby was in trouble, at any cost I couldn't afford to lose him

Everyone present was trying their best & trying to figure out how could we rescue tuffy as early as possible

The grills were hard to cut, were made of heavy metal & were thick as well

The grills were so strong and thick if we tried to cut it with any manual cutter it would take us 3-4 hrs

But to save tuffy it was required to cut the grills as early as possible

So we urgently needed the machine which was used to cut it, then it would be done in just 2 to 3 minutes

Tuffy still was crying loudly

And watching him in so much pain was horrible for me too

My dad spoke our society watchman uncle he immediately called one of his friend who was perfect in the fabrication work

But he didn't received the call as it was late night he might be in sleep after 4 calls that fabrication man called to our watchman

Watchman uncle told him how urgently we needed him and he agreed to come immediately for the sake of humanity

Then khurana uncle came. He was a retired kernel of Indian army, he saw tuffy in pain

Tuffy was so scared that even if we just touch him he was screaming, it was very bad day for every one of us.

Khurna uncle was brave. He was confident that he won't harm tuffy

There was a large opening at the middle of the gate khurana uncle and every one of us knew if we could pull tuffy's neck a bit downwards we could rescue him safely

But it was matter of pain, I couldn't see him in this much pain

Khurana uncle held tuffy's mouth in his right hand and watchmen uncle tried to expand the grill with the help of metal rode by placing it diagonally opposite between the two grills in which tuffy's neck was stuck.

Between this all the time I was assisting khurana uncle and my dad to help them rescue tuffy as I was kid they took the whole responsibility to rescue him.

Khurana uncle was standing from outside of the gate and dad then held tuffy from inside

Khurana uncle pulled tuffy gradually downwards and simultaneously dad did the same from inside

He screamed ...

But he was rescued

Yes khurana uncle saved his life.

I was in full of tears but this time the tears were of happiness I thanked god for everything that day and I started believing in more in god.

And as soon as he was rescued he jumped into my arms straightaway and sat in my lap all the time, everyone there witnessed our love for each other

Everyone clapped of khurana uncle for his bravery without him this could not be done easily.

" The pleasure is mine thank you everyone" said khurana uncle

And aniket your puppy is lovely I watch him every day when you take him out for a walk.

Take care of him son.

And khurana uncle went to his house as he was feeling very sleepy, he was very disciplined about his time and sleep

At that point of time I noticed something more

The thing is no one in our colony knew khurana uncle much, as he was very strict no one tried to do so

But at that night he came & he rescued tuffy which none of us expected from him

Since that day I would respect khurana uncle a lot he came like god for tuffy.

Dad; we need to take more care of tuffy from now onwards

Yes dad I will, I replied

The very next day dad called the fabrication peoples and they attached the nets to our main gate so that tuffy wont stuck again at any cost.

And I made sure there is no such thing that will hurt tuffy, even if anytime we are not with him

That time I understood, it is not that you have a puppy but you have to take care as much as you would take care of a human baby.

Since that incident tuffy would always recognize khurana uncle afterall he saved his life.

After this many days went on I would take tuffy to goga baba hills located near our house just 3-4 kms away and would just sit with tuffy there mesmerizing and feeling the life

Tuffy showed me the true meaning of life, my journey would be nothing without him he was such important to me

But as it is said nothing is permanent in life and we really don't know what the day bring us.

CHAPTER NINE

# He left me alone

The new morning, can't expect what the day would bring to you.

Mom opens the curtain of window, the early morning rays of the sun wakes me up

I woke up, morning mom

Good morning aniket

I was not completely woke up still stood up and went to the living room, opened the door

Tuffy was playing with his toy chewing it badly; just made sure he is alright and went back inside.

I got ready for school

Mom; tuffy became so good now he looks more healthier , his color tone has changed he looks so cute, Anyone who sees him will surely mesmerize.

Yess correct, dad replied

I was listening to this conversation and I too admired but there was no time for me to talk hence as soon as I finished my breakfast I went to school.

Till this everything seemed to be normal but you never know what the day will bring you

***

As in the morning I use to go to school, dad use to go to office & my sisters had their college and mom used to be busy in her daily routine work as she was housewife.

So there use to be no one to take tuffy out for a walk.

Tuffy use to get bored when I was not there at home he use to just wait for me to come back from school.

That's the reason why we started to let him go his own for a walk for 15-20 min, as he also became familiar with our street dogs he use to enjoy a bit with them, and he himself use to come back within time.

So everything was going in place

But that day tuffy didn't came back

Two hours passed mom thought he must be somewhere in the colony only as she was busy in her work she didn't thought much about it

Now 3 hours passed, mom checked for tuffy. He was not there in the house nor was in the colony

When I came back home;

It looked very strange to me there was no one to receive me on the gate tuffy always use to welcome me home.

I searched for him in our compound called him by his name but no reply came.

I got worried now

Mom where is tuffy?

He didn't came back aniket, mom didn't wanted to say but what else would she do

What how's this possible?

I was shivering

I didn't stop, I took my bicycle and searching colony by colony

While the tears flowing through my eyes I was driving bicycle

I shouted in every corner of our colony as well as searched in colonies beside our colony

Tuffy where are you?

Tuffy I am here

But got no response

Tears continued to flow even if I tried to stop

I madly searched for him, but I couldn't find him......!

Mom was waiting on the main door for me, mom had already informed dad

I came home after 2 hrs, fully devastated

Dad was already present at home

I cried in the lap of mom

Don't worry aniket tuffy will come back, mom said

Yess aniket your mother is right dogs never forget their house he will surely come back soon and if not we are going to find him out, dad said.

Between all this Julie aunty one of our neighbor, she told mom she saw a little boy holding tuffy and that boy must have robbed tuffy she said.

But she wasn't confirm that dog was tuffy as there is always possibility of same appearance between the dogs

But now it was confirmed that dog was tuffy as he was missing

But this was very unfortunate at least Julie aunty could have checked once then the situation would have been different.

Have faith in Mahadev son tuffy will surely come back, Mom said

My family was a great devotee of lord Mahadev and always will be

That day I cried a lot, I prayed to Mahadev, I begged to all the gods please send my tuffy back to me I cannot live without him.

Every single moment I spent with him was continuously coming in front of my eyes

However I didn't lose hopes

I again took my bicycle and went on to check for him

I asked every shopkeeper that came in my way if they had seen any white colored tone dog

I searched a lot then after sometime I thought of going to the place where I saw him 1$^{st}$ time.

I went to the garden it was a bit away from home still I thought if that boy whoever stole tuffy

If tuffy somehow escaped from there he would definitely come till here

There was a grocery shop beside the garden, I went there

Hello uncle

Yes boy what do you want?

Uncle have you seen any white colored tone dog here, actually he is lost someone robbed him

No, he replied very annoyingly

Ok thankyou

While I turned around he laughed

I could hear the sound of laughing

I knew people will laugh on me

But at this point what else was more important than tuffy, I had to find him and I was ready to do anything to get him back.

It was very hot outside 36c to 38c and I had no water bottle with me my body was dehydrating I was able to feel it.

But I didn't cared about anything at that point I just wanted tuffy back

I came home with full of tears

Couldn't find him today also

Mom hugged me, don't worry he will come back

I could see in the eyes of my sisters, mom and dad

Their eyes were moist to see tuffy again

But for me they won't express it I knew

I was feeling the vibes of our house they were not the same

Probably these were I could call the dark days of my life

I prayed, prayed day & night please mahadev save my child wherever he is keep him safe

CHAPTER TEN

# Life without tuffy

I went to the school next day with 0 percent interest in doing anything, Life without tuffy was very difficult and like hell to me.

I sat in one corner in my classroom just looking outside the window into the sky, my teacher understood something is wrong with me it was supriya ma'am our mathematics teacher.

I was sitting alone on that bench maam came to me and she sat beside me I did not know she was sitting beside

Aniket what happened beta everything alright?

I was a bit shocked

No maam, I am alright

She was a young lady understood my pain when my classmate and a best friend nikhil explained her what had happened

After the lecture maam came and hugged me and said everything will be fine don't worry, and yes that hug gave me a bit strength.

But deep inside I was losing hopes, this thing was draining me from inside I felt like nothing has left in my life.

Nikhil my best friend knew already everything & was kind enough for giving me strength during the school timings

He used to crack jokes in front of me to make me feel better but I was constantly thinking about tuffy.

Six days passed nothing seemed to be ok I was losing hopes & was broken from inside, my eyes were moist to see tuffy

Every time I thought of him tears would come in my eyes, the kind of bond I had with him &the affection for him was on different level

At that time I understood true meaning of love

And the lesson learnt from it was "life is not easy..........!"

This was the $7^{th}$ day without tuffy, I woke up got ready for school

I became almost a different personality an ambitionless person. Just around one week before, life was so good and happy suddenly life got changed

The things which used to make me happy suddenly they meant nothing to me.

I stopped expecting anything from my life, I lost all the hopes I left it all on god

CHAPTER ELEVEN

# He came back

It was English period and I was again sitting on the same bench beside the window, physically I was in class but mentally somewhere else

While I was watching outside the window the sky looked a bit different that day there were clouds all around, suddenly the sun raise emerged and fell on my eyes giving a hope and some positive vibes as well. That was the time I felt like something good will happen soon. Wasn't knowing what will happen but it gave me strength, hope and much needed positive vibes.

It was 1 o'clock bell ran and students hurried to go to their home while on the other side I wasn't much excited.

I reached home, had my meal but not a full meal, food was not been swallowed by me

Within those seven days mom recognized I lost a few kg's weight which wasn't a good sign, my parents were worried about my health not just physical health but also mentally I was stressed a lot.

My papa had even taken an appointment for counseling, as I wasn't talking to anyone

I used to just sit and won't reply much of comments, they were really worried.

However I was feeling quite normal and relaxed this day I was continuously getting good vibes like something good will happen soon.

Papa was in his office I & both my sisters were at home however mom was getting ready for a kitty party which was organized at her friend's house.

The kitty party was arranged at renuka aunty's house who was one of moms close friend. Renuka aunty's house was beside the garden and this was the same garden where I 1$^{st}$ time met tuffy

Mom told around 10 to 12 ladies were coming for the party, Julie aunty who was our neighbor was also invited for the same party so mom and Julie aunty went together.

Mom went at 4PM and I had no other plans and thus I decided to go to sleep for some time

*At renuka aunty's house:*

What happened asha you are looking worried? One of my mom's friends asked her.

Mom told her friends at the party about me and tuffy & how my behavior was changed since the time tuffy was gone

Don't take tension asha, aniket will be alright it's just a matter of a few days. He will definetly cope up with the things

Yes he should now it's been seven days now. (Mom in worrying state of mind)

The kitty party was now over it was around 7PM mom and Julie aunty were on their way to home. They both went to the party walking.

While walking towards home mom was discussing something with Julie aunty thereafter mom realized there's something continuously touching her legs from backside.

As soon as mom looked down towards her sandal mom was stunned and she had tears in her eyes

Yes it was none other than my "tuffy"

Mom just could not believe this was like a movie story.

Tuffy was dancing and jumping on mom's saree he was on the clouds he knew at last he found his family.

So many days and nights he lived alone it must have been so difficult for him.

Mom took tuffy in her arms like a small baby and took him home straight away

*At home:*

And there I was at home silent doing my stuff probably my school assignments and all. And all the day I felt like something is going to happen soon and here comes the right time.

I heard the sound of our main gate I was in our living room saw mom through the window but couldn't see tuffy as it was dark outside

I opened the living room door

And ................!

Awwaaaaaaaaaa ......!

I was shocked, stunned

Tears started flowing through my eyes I just couldn't believe anything at that time

what all was happening

I was asking questions to myself

Is this a movie story or something?

All the emotions which I carried through this seven days together came outside, I felt as if god himself reunited both of us

Mahadev heard my prayers for sure

As soon as tuffy saw me he jumped off moms arm and came to me dancing and jumping all around me, he was still shivering

I took him in my arms just holded him tightly for 2 min's

My whole family got emotional after meeting tuffy

People in our colony came especially to meet tuffy they were also shocked to see him again after so many days, as if it was a movie story

God reunited us again and there were only happy days after that.

CHAPTER TWELVE

# Life after losing him

Tuffy lived for about 8 years after that he was an important part of my life today also his memories make me smile a lot

Today in 2021 there is no tuffy no papa in my life both left me but I am still hoping wherever they are they both might be living together and happy

And still hoping to meet them again in heaven

But I do have all the happy memories with both of them

Love you tuffy

Love you papa

And I miss you both a lot be happy wherever you both are.

***Will you meet me again tuffy?***

Printed by Libri Plureos GmbH in Hamburg,
Germany